Happy Anniversary!

Remember That?

Content by Ivy Nufwards (2022)

Cover Photo by Tumisu

Happy Anniversary!

________________ is the date

that we first ______________________.

Happy Anniversary!

________________ is the date

that we first ______________________.

Happy Anniversary!

________________ is the date

that we first ______________________.

(Insert photo, drawing, or keepsake here)

(Insert photo, drawing, or keepsake here)

When you smile at me,

it makes me feel:

(Insert photo, drawing, or keepsake here)

When I look deep into your eyes,

I'm thinking:

(Insert photo, drawing, or keepsake here)

What I love about your hair is:

(Insert photo, drawing, or keepsake here)

Remember the time we drove all the

way to _______________________________?

Just so we could :

(Insert photo, drawing, or keepsake here)

My favorite dream that I have had about you is:

(Insert photo, drawing, or keepsake here)

Remember when we went to

that live performance,

_______________________________________?

And then this happened:

(Insert photo, drawing, or keepsake here)

I think about us whenever
I hear this song:

(Insert photo, drawing, or keepsake here)

If we actually walked off the pages
of a love story, you would be the
character who…

And, I would be the character who…

(Insert photo, drawing, or keepsake here)

I used to tell my friends that you:

(Did you know that?)

(Insert photo, drawing, or keepsake here)

Remember when I was so upset

about_______________________________?

And then you said:

(I'll never forget that.)

(Insert photo, drawing, or keepsake here)

I once almost got you

----

as a gift, but then I changed my
mind because:

(Insert photo, drawing, or keepsake here)

Nobody makes

----

like you do!

(Insert photo, drawing, or keepsake here)

If I could take you on vacation
anywhere, I'd love to take you to

_____________________________________,

because:

(Insert photo, drawing, or keepsake here)

You make my heart beat faster
when you:

(I mean, it beats really fast!)

(Insert photo, drawing, or keepsake here)

When I suddenly hear your voice
inside my head, it is saying:

(Insert photo, drawing, or keepsake here)

It's a good thing we didn't meet any sooner than we did,

because if we had:

(Insert photo, drawing, or keepsake here)

I'm glad I finally told you about

_________________________________,

because I really didn't need to keep

that a secret from you.

(Insert photo, drawing, or keepsake here)

(Insert photo, drawing, or keepsake here)

If reincarnation is really a thing,

I think we might have been together

in

____
(this part of the world)

during_________________________________.
(this time in history)

(Insert photo, drawing, or keepsake here)

If there is such a thing as an afterlife, I'm going to tell you this when I see you there:

(Remember that.)

(Insert photo, drawing, or keepsake here)

We go together like:

(Awwwww!)

www.ingramcontent.com/pod-product-compliance
Lightning Source LLC
Chambersburg PA
CBHW051406150726
48000CB00003B/1347